Notes by Nature

Cameron Davis

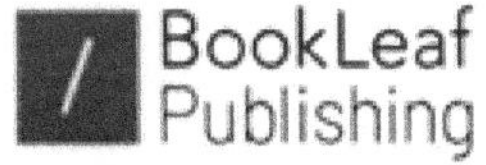

Presentation by *BookLeaf Publishing*

Web: www.bookleafpub.com

E-mail: info@bookleafpub.com

ISBN: 9789357213028

First edition 2023

WATER

Slick and smooth
Undefined
Always flowing
Clear blue or crystal clear
Cool and refreshing
Our source of life
What keeps our skin glowing and plants growing
Water is what we need, love, and waste

CLOUDS

I look up
I see white looming over me
So white pure and fluffy
Different textures
Overwhelming beauty
Contrast of white on blue make the sky seem so
magical
The clouds reach beyond the sky's limit

MOON

Circles round the earth
Every night, every year,
Full, crescent and half
Glowing
Illuminating
Enchanting
The moon with its changing sizes and shapes
It's ever so hypnotizing glow in the night sky

TIME

Seconds, minutes, hours,
Days, weeks, and months
Years that go on
The world revolving around the sun
Time passes us by
Taller, stronger, faster
Gray hair, wrinkles form
Never stopping
Always moving
Many changes come with passage of time

ICE CREAM

Cold and creamy
Sweet with bits of fruit
Multitude of flavors one could chose from
The cold melts in your mouth
Once it hits your tongue
Too melted or too cold
There is no such thing as a perfect day for ice
cream
Every day is perfect for ice cream

NOURISHMENT

Carrots, cake, or chips
We love food, always craving it
The sweet or the savory
The salty and the tart
Sometimes we yearn for more
Other times, we can't stand another bite
Some are good for us, giving us life
Others are harmful, clogging our bodies
Consume more of the good
Only a little of the bad
Because vitamins and minerals are the essential tools

SMART(?) PHONE

Hypnotic,
Always reaching for one more second of it
Our eyes always following the glow of its screen
Tapping, scrolling, and swiping
Unaware to the issues that lie within that glass
Laughing
Anger
Liking and sending to a friend
Thirty minutes
Two hours
Caught up in the endless scroll
Enough is never enough

THE INTERNET

Looming
Watching
Taking notes
Not in the dark shadows
Not in a deserted alley
But in your pockets
Or maybe even in your backpack
Always watching
What we buy
What we read
Maybe I don't feel too well
Let me look that up
Always collecting, compiling, sorting
Creating a profile
Saving
Always saving....

BOOKS

Every letter and each word
Conveys a story
Each page you turn
Tells a different part of that story
Each chapter
Adds on to that story
Shelves and shelves hold a thousand chapters
Each one telling a different story for generations
to come

MONEY

Work for it
Borrow it
Sometimes they steal it
Beg for it
Commit crime for it
Always wanting more and more
The lush greenery of money
Pain and hurt it causes when we don't have
enough
Loss and hunger that results when we don't have
any
Envy and greed take over when we desire too
much of it
So enticing, so necessary

BLOOM

Lush greenery fills our earth
Roses, leaves, and bushes
Crunching and stepping
On the dead ones that fall to the ground
From the green buds to the full bloom flowers
Gardens full to the one small leaf in a forest
Life starts in a bud
Then blossoms into full bloom

EXPLORE AND DISCOVER

So beautiful and green
The world with its blue ocean
And its green mountains
New wonders that haven't been discovered
Remain undiscovered
Beneath the ocean
To the ice capped hills
Explore
Uncover

THE SUN

The sun rises and sets
Light and beauty emanate from her
She kisses our plants
And gives life and warmth
She decides our seasons
What we will wear
Will we go swimming or skiing
That depends on if we are far or near
Is she covered by clouds?
Or bold and in full view?
She once told us the time
But she always tells us so much more
The Sun
She has the answers

BIRTHDAY

Family giving love and hugs
Surrounded by singing friends
This day
Only once a year
Joy and fun memories being created
Presents and cake
For living another 365 days
Congratulations

WINTER SNOW

Layer on layer we dress
Each one separating us from the bitter cold
White snow flurries
Falling one snowflake at a time from the sky
Each one collecting into a mountain
Where people find happiness
Sliding down millions of snowflakes

SUNSET

Sinking down past our view
Depriving the sky of it's lively blue
Looming over with an inky black
And sprinkles of white now dot the sky
Darkness
Surrounding everything
And new creatures come out

FALL

A new time of the year is coming
Brown takes center stage
Splashes of yellow and red
And plenty of orange too
The comforting cooling feeling
Hearing the brown crunchy leaves beneath our
feet
All while knowing
It's just a new season coming along

RED

You're so bright and flashy and bold
Cherries, tomatoes and strawberries
My favorite items of clothing
The fastest cars on the road
Ladybugs on my porch
The roses in my garden
Your bright presence can't help but make others stare
You're in my blood
Inside and outside, I can't escape you

PLANES TRAINS AUTOMOBILES

Travel to work, school, home
Vacation, errands, meetings
Far away lands or up the street
But the means of our journey aren't always so
great
Exhaust and smoke and pollution
We arrive to our destination
But eventually our destination won't look so
pretty

DRILLING

Pump pump pump
Drill
Frack
Pump pump pump
Out of the earth
Into our cars and into our machines
The sky is now cloudy
And the air smells badly
Pollution
Contamination
Wild animals scatter and run
Oh no is that a spill?
Clean it up
The time has come
To find a better way

EMPIRE

He sits comfortably
Up atop his mountain of money
Whirring of the conveyor belt
Buzzing of the gears
In and out of his factory
Items come and go
The only finished product
His heart cares about
Is the money
The green outshines
Out dazzles
Over glamorizes
The remaining factors
He turns a blind eye to
Blind to the damage of our oceans
Blind to the landfills
That will soon be overflowing
Blind to the smoky skies
Filled with pollution
The fortune calls his name
Much louder than
The Earth cries for help
In false attempts to show compassion
The blame now shifts...
The consumer

It's all our fault
Reduce, Reuse, Recycle
Turn off that faucet
Hit the light switch
How are we able to enjoy life,
While killing the only things that lets us live
What purpose does money serve,
When our Earth has nothing left to give?